CRISPER TRAY
PIZZA
COOKBOOK

Crispy Crust Complete Air Fryer Style Nonstick Copper Basket, Chef Recommended Baking Recipes for Your Oven Stovetop or Grill for Wood Fire Method Healthy Cooking at Home

LEONA STELLENBERG

Crisper Tray Pizza Recipe Cookbook

LEGAL

DISCLAIMER: This book is independently published by, and is **not** affiliated with, sponsored by, or endorsed by any of the products mentioned in this book. All other company and product names are the trademarks of their respective owners.

This information contained in this book is for entertainment purposes only. The content represents the opinion of the author and is based on the author's personal experience and observations. The author does not assume any liability whatsoever for the use of or inability to use any or all information contained in this book, and accepts no responsibility for any loss or damages of any kind that may be incurred by the reader as a result of actions arising from the use of the information in this book. Use this information at your own risk. No part of this book may be reproduced or transmitted in any form or by any means, electronic or mechanical, including photocopying, recording, or by any information storage or retrieval system, without express written permission from the author, except in the case of brief quotations embodied in critical articles and reviews – or except by a reviewer who may quote brief passages in a review.

Respective authors hold all copyrights not held by the publisher

NOTE: Some of the recipes in this book include raw eggs. Raw eggs may contain bacteria. It is recommended that you purchase certified salmonella-free eggs from a reliable source and store them in the refrigerator. You should not feed raw eggs to babies or small kids. Likewise, pregnant women, elderly persons, or those with a compromised immune system should not eat raw eggs. Neither the author nor the publisher claims responsibility for adverse effects resulting from the use of the recipes and/or information found within this book.

The author reserves the right to make any changes he or she deems necessary to future versions of the publication to ensure its accuracy.

COPYRIGHT © 2018

All Rights Reserved.

Published in The United States of America

ns
INTRODUCTION

Pizza has evolved since it appeared on American shores in the late 1800s. The specialty food, we so love today, came with the mass immigration of Southern Italian immigrants. Pizza was created in Naples for the working class, and it stayed at home with the Italian immigrant families until the neighborhood pizzeria was opened.

In 2018, pizza comes in many different shapes, sizes and styles. From the brick oven to the franchise fast food style pizza and even to your kitchen, there are so many different ways to be creative with your pie that it is a wonder how universal the dish has become. When ordering or making a pizza there are so many different options. Some people like it plain and simple, with just cheese and sauce, and others like to fill it up with different types of toppings. No matter how you like your pizza, everyone can agree that it is a very unique and tasty dish that they could never live without.

We have to ask, what makes a pizza truly a pizza? Is it the crust? Is it the sauce? The toppings? Or is it all of the above? This has been a topic for discussion for years and some have argued that the crust is what makes a pizza. You can choose from New Haven Style, New York Style, Chicago Deep Dish, Louisiana Style, Neapolitan, thin crust and more. The same goes for the different styles of pizza sauce: Tomato sauce, pine nut sauce, pumpkin and beet sauce and more. No matter what you believe what makes a pizza, it is great to be able to have so many different options to choose from.

People usually worry about whether pizza is a healthy choice. Some people find that eating pizza puts on calories and makes them gain weight. However, there are a lot of healthier options that can be used nowadays. Ones that don't compromise the taste. With the creation of the whole wheat crust, cracker crust, and even the cauliflower crust, people who have allergies or are health conscious can still enjoy pizza like the rest of the world.

One of the best things about the evolution of pizza is the many ways it can be cooked. This particular book focuses on the Crisper Basket/Tray and how it can make a pizza that surpasses anything you have ever tasted before – minus the oils and butter that you would normally cook with. So, sit back, watch and be dazzled with what we are about to show you!

Crisper Tray Pizza Recipe Cookbook

TABLE OF CONTENTS

Legal	2
Introduction	3
Table Of Contents	4
The Crisper For Pizza... No Way!	7
Make It Work For You	7
What? You Say.	7
Give Your Guest A Reason To Brag!	7
They'll Be Coming Back For More	7
Designed With Intelligence!	8
Dual Combination Cooking Power	8
How It Works	8
Texture Of The Base Of The Crust	8
Something To Keep In Mind	9
The Magic Of Crisper Crust!	10
A Little Oil To Brush The Crust	10
Master The Craft	10
How Crispy Is Up To You!	10
Crisper Care	11
Cage Strong	11
Easy Cleaning	11
Crisper Storage	11
For The Love Of Pizza	12
Any Pizza You've Ever Wanted	12
Everyone Loves Pizza	12
Now That's A Mouth Full	12
Getting Creative	13
There's More On The Menu Than Pizza!	13
Use Your Imagination!	13
Share The Experience	13
The Crisper Pro's Know	14
Never Too Much Garlic!	14
If In Doubt...Put It In The Crust	14
Flavoring Favorites	14
Before You Go Further...	15
Make Sure You Get Yours!	15

Super Yummy Crust Section: 16
Rising Pizza Dough	17
Thin Crust Pizza Crust	19
Cracker Pizza Crust	21
St. Louis Sytle Pizza Crust	23

Section 8: Healthier Crust: 25
Califlower Crust	26
Zucchini Crust	28
Butternut Squash Crust	29
Whole-Wheat Dough	31
Flatbread (Gluten Free) Pizza Crust	33
Beet Style Pizza Crust	35
Eggplant Pizza Crust	37
Sweet Potato Pizza Crust	38

Section 9: Combination Of Sauces: 40
Pine Nutty Pesto Sauce	41
Creamy Bechamel Sauce	43
Zesty Salsa Recipe	45
Sweet And Tangy Barbeque Sauce	46
Savory Pumpkin Puree Sauce	48
Hum For Hummus Style Pizza Sauce	49
No Tomato In This Tomato Sauce	50
Black Olive Tapenade Sauce	52
Carrot Chili Paste Sauce	53
Garlic And Olive Oil Sauce	55
Peppery Jelly Pizza Style Sauce	56
Miso And Macadamian Nut Ricotta Sauce	57
Caramelized Onion Sauce	58
Go Back To The Basics Tomato Sauce	60
Middle Eastern Zaatar Sauce	62
Thai Peanut Sauce	63
Japanese Lime Wasabi Sauce	64
Garlic Aioli Pizza Sauce	65
Basil And Sun-Dried Tomato Sauce	66
Lower In Fat Alfredo Sauce	68
Fiery Spanish Romesco Sauce	70

Section 10: Pizza Toppings / Let's Get Creative: 72
The Original Neopolitan	72
Sunny California Style	73
Chicago – Thin Crust Style	74
Greek Style Pizza	75
St. Louis Style	76
Thai Chicken Style Pizza	78

Mexican Style Pizza	79
New Orleans Muffaletta Style Pizza	80
Hawaiian Style Pizza	82
Pissaladiere French Style Pizza	83
Salad Sytle Pizza	84
Miami-Cuban Style Pizza	85
German Sausage Pizza	86
White Clam Style Pizza	87
Breakfast Style Pizza	88
Chicken Alfredo Style Pizza	89
Meat Lovers Style Pizza	90
Veggie Style Pizza	91
Everything Style Pizza	92
Grilled Everything Style Pizza	93
Charts For Home Cooking	**94**
Food Temperatures For Safe Heating, Danger Chilling & Freezing Zones!	94
Meat Baking Chart Temperatures!	95
Next On The List!	**96**
Here's What You Do Now...	96
About The Author	**97**
Free Books!!!	**98**
Make Sure You Get Yours!	98
Crisper Tray Pizza Cookbook Recipes & Notes:	99
Crisper Tray Pizza Cookbook Recipes & Notes:	100

THE CRISPER FOR PIZZA... NO WAY!

MAKE IT WORK FOR YOU
The Crisper Basket/Tray is a device that can be used to make any type of pizza that you are interested in. From Chicago Deep Dish to Thin Crust, you can choose the crust of your choice and make this cooking utensil work for you!

WHAT? YOU SAY.
Just hear us out. We promise that we will have you sold in no time. The Crisper Basket/Tray is a great way to create a pie that doesn't require oils or butter when you cook it. It is one of the best ways to cook the pizza in the oven or air fry we should say.

GIVE YOUR GUEST A REASON TO BRAG!
Using the Crisper Basket/Tray at your next pizza party gives your guests another reason to brag. This is one of the best and innovative ways to create your next pizza pie and you can do it in the oven without having to use oils or butter to keep the dough from sticking to the pan. The air fryer cooks the pizza in its own oils and it makes it marvelous.

Pizza has many different flavor components, when added to the right dough you can make something you will want to keep making over and over again. Crust, sauce and toppings all have different types of flavors that work with different palates and even ingredients that strengthen the flavor in any type of pizza. So, go to your kitchen and let us get started and make some pizzas.

THEY'LL BE COMING BACK FOR MORE
Once your friends, neighbors and family members taste the types of pizza that come out of the Crisper Basket/Tray they will be coming back every time they have pizza on the brain. But, this time they will be asking you to teach them how to make these succulent recipes themselves.

When you make these pies, do not skimp on the toppings. Deciding which ones work best with your dish can make all the difference? And, not just on your palate, but on your next dinner or dessert party, as well.

DESIGNED WITH INTELLIGENCE!

DUAL COMBINATION COOKING POWER

The Crisper Basket/Tray kit consists of a non-stick mesh basket that lies on top of a non-stick cookie sheet. The mesh basket is coated with ceramic combined with a stainless-steel rim that allows the heat of the oven to pass through and circulate 360 degrees, which cooks all sides of the pizza at the same time.

The great thing about this air fryer is that the air that circulates around the pizza makes the dough crispier than you have ever had it before and it leaves all of the other ingredients tender and juicy.

If you decide that you don't want to cook the pie in the basket, you can place the dough on the non-stick cookie sheet, which will still cook the pizza in its own juices. The baking sheet also catches any crumbs, grease, or drippings from the mesh basket. This helps keep your oven clean and safe while cooking your food just the way that you want.

HOW IT WORKS

This perfect crisper air fryer is a great way to cook the dough of any pie and make it as crisp as you could possibly want it. The non-stick ceramic coating of the Crisper Basket/Tray allows you to cook without butter, oil or any other chemicals that keep your food from sticking to the basket or baking sheet. Now you can cook while reducing calories and fat.

The oil-less air-baking that the Crisper Basket/Tray provides is an excellent alternative to cooking the conventional way, and it helps those who are very interested in reducing cholesterol or avoiding extra calories. Using the air fryer helps conserve the amounts of vitamins in your food that are usually lost in traditional cooking.

However...in some of these crust recipes we have you to brush light oil because we know there are some of you who like your crust Super, Extra Crispy!

TEXTURE OF THE BASE OF THE CRUST

The great thing about the Crisper Basket/Tray is that it creates a great texture on the bottom of your crust. The base of your crust will be cooked all around and made to perfection. This doesn't matter if you are using thin, deep dish or New York style crust, the basket will cook the crust just the way you like it.

The base of the crust will be cooked all the way through, but can be just as doughy or as crispy as you want it. This makes the Crisper Basket/Tray the best way to make pizza. You will love how this utensil makes your crust feel and taste in your mouth.

SOMETHING TO KEEP IN MIND

Some crusts may not work as well in the crisper tray because of the cage like surface. Some of these crusts will have to be made on the cookie sheet that comes with your instead. These crusts include:

- Cauliflower Crust
- Zucchini Crust
- Butternut Squash Crust
- Whole-Wheat Dough
- Flatbread (Gluten Free) Pizza Crust
- Beet Style Pizza Crust
- Eggplant Pizza Crust
- Sweet Potato Pizza Crust

THE MAGIC OF CRISPER CRUST!

A LITTLE OIL TO BRUSH THE CRUST

We often cook with butter, oils and other chemicals to keep our food from sticking onto the pan, baking sheet or even pizza peel. Those tend to add unneeded calories to our meal, especially if we want to eat healthy. However, there are times we use oils to add a little bit of flavor to the meal. In that case, olive oil, avocado and other natural oils are great to use in such cases.

With the non-stick Crisper Basket/Tray you can use the oils to add more flavor to your crust. Just brush it all over your pizza dough for some added color and flavor. You will not regret how great it tastes.

MASTER THE CRAFT

Making the perfect dough is an exact art. It is not necessarily the ingredients that go into the dough that makes the dough special, it is how you handle it. Personally kneading your dough with your hands, gives you that one on one personal connection with your dough. It helps you master it to the perfect type of consistency.

Once you master your dough then you can choose all of the other ingredients that you would like to go on your pie and put the Crisper Basket/Tray into the oven. Since you're becoming the master of pizza making, it is important that you check the dough so that you can cook it to the perfect consistency!

HOW CRISPY IS UP TO YOU!

On every pizza recipe, we are told how long we are supposed to cook our pizza crust for. What if you wanted your crust to be a little more doughy than normal, or burnt on the bottom? All of this is your choice. No one is telling you how long you should cook your crust that is totally up to you.

The Crisper Basket/Tray is the perfect cooking utensil because it allows you to cook things as crisp as you want. This includes all of the toppings, and the crust. So, start creating something great in the kitchen.

Leona Stellenberg

CRISPER CARE

CAGE STRONG

The Crisper mesh basket is 9' x 12' in size. And it can hold most sizes or weights of ingredients. It can hold any pizza dough and toppings that you want to put on your pizza. The cage is made of sturdy stainless steel and it will not break down after continuous uses.

When using the mesh basket, do not be fooled at how it looks and test it out for yourself. You will understand once you try it and realize that it is not flimsy, but made to hold all of your ingredients without falling apart. So, come and try the product today. You will not be disappointed.

EASY CLEANING

The Crisper Basket/Tray is very easy to clean. It is dishwasher safe! However, it is recommended that it be cleaned by hand. We ask that you wash it in warm water, with non- abrasive soap and a non-metallic sponge or cloth. Please make sure that the crisper cools off before you emerge it into water.

It is important to take care of the crisper so that it has a great shelf life. For instance, do not use baking soda, detergents or other harsh soaps or solutions on the crisper itself. Other than that, the Crisper Basket/Tray is very easy to clean. When rinsed off, it can be put inside the dishwasher, which gives you a faster clean up and more time to enjoy some of the other things you enjoy doing.

CRISPER STORAGE

Storing any of your cookware is a very important task. A lot of pots and pans, especially non-stick, are supposed to be stored away from others so they do not get cut or scratched, which in all reality can ruin the non-stick part of the utensil. That is one of the most important parts of the basket, and we want you to be able to use the Crisper Basket/Tray for long periods of time.

We recommend that you avoid direct exposure to other cookware, or bakeware. If you have to store with other cookware, adding a protective layer in between the other pieces can ensure the life of your Crisper Basket/Tray for years to come.

FOR THE LOVE OF PIZZA

ANY PIZZA YOU'VE EVER WANTED
Have you ever dreamed of creating your own type of pizza? Well now is your chance. You can be as creative as you want to be, and have some fun in the kitchen. The recipes we provide in this book give you the opportunity to choose a different type of crust, sauce and toppings than you are normally used too.

Sometimes we eat what we are comfortable with, and we are afraid of trying new things. The great thing about pizza is that everything tastes good on top of dough. You can mix match non-traditional crusts and sauces, and even toppings. Who can tell us how to eat pizza? It is our right to be creative! We encourage you to do that!

EVERYONE LOVES PIZZA
Everyone loves pizza!!! Let us say that again, everyone loves pizza!! With that being said this book is created to make some of the best pizzas in the world. This book is created to help you become more creative in the kitchen and to get out of your pizza comfort zone. It is okay to eat more than just pepperoni or sausage on pizza. It is okay to stem out and live a little. Use this book to give you a chance to play around in the kitchen. Bring in the kids and the husband and make pizza creating time with the family. We bet it is something that they will love and want to do again and again.

NOW THAT'S A MOUTH FULL
Fit these delightful pies into your mouth. Get creative and make different ones. We recommend inventing an international pizza night and make pizzas from Spain, France, Mexico, America, Thailand, and Italy. A lot of these recipes use ingredients that are known in those. Pizza is one of the few dishes that have brought people together all over the world. When visiting different cities, states and countries, you will find that they have their own version of pizza, which may not be as different as you think. Trying new types of pizza can open up your palette to different types of tastes.

GETTING CREATIVE

THERE'S MORE ON THE MENU THAN PIZZA!
You can use the Crisper Basket/Tray basket on the outdoor grill or in the oven. That means that you can create tons of other types of food inside the basket. It does not necessarily have to be pizza.

The Crisper Basket/Tray can be used to bake fry foods such as chicken, vegetables, and even ribs or a whole ham. There is nothing that cannot be cooked inside the basket or on the baking sheet. Small thin flatbreads or even mini pizzas can be made inside the baking sheet. No matter what you are in the mood for tonight, the Crisper Tray is great for most or all your cooking needs.

USE YOUR IMAGINATION!
Making pizza should always be a fun experience. Look at our recipes as a guide to make pizza and then go from there. Our recipes are just ideas, but if they are not exactly what you want, it is okay to start to use your imagination and create your own.

Think about all of the great ingredients that you love to eat. Ask yourself if they will be good on a pizza. And then go for it. You will never know what it tastes like unless you try it. The whole idea of cooking is to experiment in the kitchen and create something that people have never had before. So, have some fun and start creating!

SHARE THE EXPERIENCE
One of the great things about cooking is to be able to share it with those you love. And making pizza is one of those experiences. Bring in the whole family and create different types of crusts. See if the kids want to make a deep dish, stuff crust or even a thin crust. They might want to make more than one pizza with different types of crusts, sauces and toppings.

Go wild with the toppings and let them put whatever they want on their pizza. After all, you are trying to show them that they can be creative and innovative in the kitchen. Let them know that it is okay to try new types of foods or tastes. This will ensure that they will not be picky eaters, especially when it comes to their pizzas.

THE CRISPER PRO'S KNOW

NEVER TOO MUCH GARLIC!

Garlic is great to cook with, especially when it comes to Italian food – like pizza. What if I told you that garlic was more beneficial for you than just to enhance the flavor on your pizza? Garlic is actually really healthy for your and is great for your immune system.

Garlic is high in Manganese, Vitamin B6, Vitamin C, Selenium and fiber. It also contains decent amounts of calcium, copper, potassium, phosphorus, iron and Vitamin B1; as well as low in caloric intake.

So, go ahead and put as much garlic on your pizza as you want. There is never too much garlic, unless you want to kiss someone right away. Then you might want to chew a stick of gum first.

IF IN DOUBT...PUT IT IN THE CRUST

Sometimes it can be difficult to figure out what ingredients you want to put on your pie or there might be too much. Well, we live in the world of stuffed crust and if you are in doubt of putting any ingredient on top of the crust, have you ever thought of stuffing it inside the crust?

We have seen different types of pizza makers stuff cheese in the crust, but that is not the only ingredient that tastes good inside the top of the crust or in the middle of the crust itself. Try stuffing some sausage, cheese and olives inside the crust for some added flavor. You might find that it is one of the best things you have ever done!

FLAVORING FAVORITES

We all know what we like to eat. There are certain types of foods or flavors that we go to every time we cook or order something in a restaurant, and this is okay. Putting these flavors together in your mind can make a great type of pizza.

For instance, if you love eating flatbread, with lamb, onions, olives, feta and tzatziki sauce, then you should try these Mediterranean ingredients on a flatbread style pizza. These are some of the ideas we recommend when you start using our unique cookbook.

Leona Stellenberg

BEFORE YOU GO FURTHER...

MAKE SURE YOU GET YOURS!
Monthly We Try Publishing A New Book. Be The First To Get YOUR FREE COPY!

Free Books
About Once A Month We Publish New Books
Click Here for Instant Access

Like receiving free books...I bet you do! We promote our new books to our current members so you can review our new books and give us feedback when we launch new books we are publishing! This helps us determine how we can make our books better for you, our audience! Just go to the url below and leave your name and email. We will send you a complimentary book about once a month.

CLICK HERE
for Instant Access

http://eepurl.com/ds1EjX

SUPER YUMMY CRUST SECTION:

Ask any Italian pie maker, pizza crust is more than just bread. It is the foundation of the pizza itself. A burnt, lifeless crust will kill the taste and flavor of the pizza. This is why so many different chefs perfect the way they make their crust because without it there is no pizza.

There are a lot of different ways to make dough, especially when it comes to the type of consistency that you want to achieve: traditional, pan, thin crust or even deep dish. However, the world of pizza has grown and there are so many alternative ways to make crust nowadays.

For instance, those who have gluten allergies don't have to sit this one out. You are allowed to eat pizza again: from gluten free flour, to cauliflower, zucchini or squash. You can eat your pizza and not have to worry about the guilt either. Either way you look at it, if you just want to be healthy, have a food allergy or want to try something different. Our crust section has something for everyone to enjoy.

RISING PIZZA DOUGH

Nothing is better than pizza! However, we all know that the best part of pizza is the dough! Learning how to create and perfect your dough is what is going to make your homemade pizza a success.

Total Time: 85 minutes

Makes: 6 Servings

INGREDIENTS:
Makes enough for two 10-12 inch pizzas

1 ½ cups warm water

1 package active dry yeast

3 ¾ cups bread flour

2 tbsp. olive oil

2 tsp. salt

1 tsp. sugar

DIRECTIONS:
- Equipment needed: Crisper tray, stand mixer, peel and brush (for oil)
- Preheat oven to 475.
- Pour warm water in the bowl of a standing mixer.
- Lightly pour the yeast in the water and let sit for 5 minutes, make sure the yeast has fully dissolved in the water.
- Mix in the flour, salt, sugar, and olive oil. Using the mixing paddle, place the setting on low speed for 1 minute.
- Replace the paddle with the dough hook attachment and knead the pizza dough on low for 8 minutes.

- Sprinkle olive oil in a large bowl and coat the dough with the oil. Cover the dough with plastic wrap/set in a warm setting for no less than 1 ½ hours.
- Punch the dough down to release the air.
- Separate the dough into two and roll each half into a ball.
- Let rest into two separate bowls, lightly covered for 15 minutes
- Sprinkle the peel with cornmeal
- Flatten the dough on the peel to fit into the crisper tray.
- Lift the dough to create a lip at the edges and place into the crisper tray.
- Brush the top lightly with olive oil.
- With your fingers push dents into the surface to prevent bubbling.
- Now start prepping for your pizza creation.
- Choose from a combination of sauces in Section 9 pg. 40 (Recipes start on Page 41)
- Choose from our creative list of toppings in Section 10 (Starts on Page 72)

THIN CRUST PIZZA CRUST

When eating pizza, we want the ingredients to stand out. Making a really thin crust lets you have that freedom.

Total Time: 85 minutes

Makes: 4 Servings

INGREDIENTS:

Makes enough for two 10-12 inch pizzas

¾ cup lukewarm water

1 tsp. active dry yeast

2 cups unbleached all-purpose flour

¾ tsp. salt

2 tsp. olive oil, divided

DIRECTIONS:

- Equipment needed: Crisper tray, peel, stand mixer and brush (for olive oil)
- Preheat oven to 475.
- Pour warm water in the bowl of a standing mixer.
- Lightly pour the yeast in the water and let sit for 5 minutes, make sure the yeast has fully dissolved in the water.
- Mix in the flour, and salt. Using the mixing paddle, place the setting on low speed for 1 minute.
- Replace the paddle with the dough hook attachment and knead the pizza dough on low for 8 minutes.

- Sprinkle olive oil in a large bowl and coat the dough with the oil. Cover the dough with plastic wrap/set in a warm setting for no less than 1 ½ hours.
- Punch the dough down to release the air.
- Separate the dough into two and roll each half into a ball.
- Let rest into two separate bowls, lightly covered for 15 minutes
- Sprinkle the peel with cornmeal
- Flatten the dough on the peel to fit into the crisper tray.
- Use the heel of your hand, gently press down and stretch the dough until it is ¼ inch thick or less
- Lift the dough to create a lip at the edges and place into the crisper tray.
- Brush the top lightly with olive oil.
- With your fingers push dents into the surface to prevent bubbling.
- Cook for 8-12 minutes.
- Now start prepping for your pizza creation.
- Choose from a combination of sauces in Section 9 pg. 40 (Recipes start on Page 41)
- Choose from our creative list of toppings in Section 10 (Starts on Page 72)

CRACKER PIZZA CRUST

This crispy, flaky, crackly and great for the belly crust give you the chance to eat 7 more slices if you wanted to. And the best part is that the no yeast and no rise recipe makes it easier to make without compromising on the texture and flavor.

Total Time: 85 minutes

Makes: 24 Servings

INGREDIENTS:

5 tbsp. warm water

2 tsp. olive oil, divided

¼ tsp. active dry yeast

3.5 ounces bread flour

3.5 ounces bread flour

3 tbsp. semolina flour

2 tbsp. fresh rosemary, chopped

½ tsp. salt

DIRECTIONS:

› Equipment needed: Crisper tray, peel, measuring cup, and brush (for oil)

› Preheat oven to 475.

› Combine water, 1 tbsp. oil and yeast in a bowl. Let stand for 2 minutes.

› Weigh out 5 oz. bread crumbs in a measuring cup.

› Sprinkle over the yeast mixture, add the rosemary, semolina flour and salt.

› Stir together until combined.

› Knead dough on counter for 1 minutes

› Sprinkle 1 tbsp. olive oil in a large bowl and coat the dough with the oil. Cover the dough with plastic wrap and set in a warm setting for 40 minutes.

- Sprinkle the peel with cornmeal
- Flatten the dough on the peel to fit into the crisper tray.
- Place into the crisper tray.
- Brush the top lightly with olive oil.
- Cook for 5 minutes.
- Now start prepping for your pizza creation.
- Choose from a combination of sauces in Section 9 pg. 40 (Recipes start on Page 41)
- Choose from our creative list of toppings in Section 10 (Starts on Page 72)

ST. LOUIS SYTLE PIZZA CRUST

The St. Louis Style Pizza is the King of the Cracker pizza crust. Yet, we don't want you to stop there. Once you make this crust you will want to know how to make the rest of the recipe.

Total Time: 15 minutes

Makes: 12 Servings

INGREDIENTS:

Makes enough for two 10-12 inch pizzas

2 cups all-purpose flour

2 tbsp. all-purpose flour

½ tsp. salt

1 tsp. baking powder

2 tsp. olive oil

2 tsp. dark corn syrup

½ cup water

2 tbsp. water

DIRECTIONS:

> Equipment needed: Crisper tray, peel, brush (for oil)
> Preheat oven to 475.
> Mix all of the ingredients together in a bowl.
> Separate the dough into two and roll each half into a ball.
> Sprinkle the peel with cornmeal
> Flatten the dough on the peel to fit into the crisper tray.

- Lift the dough to create a lip at the edges and place into the crisper tray.
- Brush the top lightly with olive oil.
- With your fingers push dents into the surface to prevent bubbling.
- Cook for 15 minutes.
- Now start prepping for your pizza creation.
- Choose from a combination of sauces in Section 9 pg. 40 (Recipes start on Page 41)
- Choose from our creative list of toppings in Section 10 (Starts on Page 72)

SECTION 8: HEALTHIER CRUST:

Some of us feel guilty when the thought of pizza fills our minds. Or the fact that you are allergic to gluten makes you feel iffy when you think of pizza. Either way, there are healthier versions of dough that you can eat that will not make you feel guilty or mess with your allergies. We have added some of the recipes right here in this section.

When making pizza dough, there is an option to replace the white flour with another type of flour to fit your needs. For instance, you can substitute whole wheat flour, oat flour, beans (black beans or chickpeas), buckwheat flour, nut flours, spelt flour, and coconut flour to name a few.

If you have a gluten allergy finding gluten and wheat free flour is not as big as a challenge as you think. Here are a few options you can choose to replace regular flour:

- Amaranth Flour
- Arrowroot Flour,
- Banana Flour,
- Barley Flour,
- Brown Rice Flour,
- Buckwheat Flour,
- Chia Flour,
- Chickpea Flour,
- Coconut Flour,
- Coffee Flour,
- Corn Flour,
- Cornmeal,
- Hemp Flour,
- Lupine Flour,
- Maize Flour,
- Millet Flour,
- Oat Flour,
- Potato Flour,
- Potato Starch Flour,
- Quinoa Flour,
- Rye Flour (Wheat Free),
- Sorghum Flour,
- Soya Flour,
- Tapioca Flour,
- Teff Flour
- White Rice Flour

just to name a few.

Choose any of these flours to substitute regular wheat flour in making your pizza crusts or choose some of the recipes we have added below. **Note:** Please make sure to read your flour instructions to see which is the best substitute for your pizza creations!

CALIFLOWER CRUST

Cauliflower is a great food source that contains 77 percent of the recommended daily value of Vitamin C in one serving. Who knew that eating pizza could be so healthy for you?

Total Time: 60 minutes

Makes: 6 Servings

INGREDIENTS:

1 small head of cauliflower, chopped

1 cup Parmesan cheese, grated

¾ tsp. Italian Seasoning

1 garlic clove, minced

½ tsp. salt

½ tsp. pepper

1 egg

DIRECTIONS:

- Equipment needed: crisper cookie sheet, peel, parchment paper, and brush (for oil)
- Preheat oven to 475.
- Pour the chopped cauliflower in a food processor and mix until finely ground.
- Cook cauliflower in a microwave safe bowl for approximately 4-5 min.
- Pour the cauliflower onto a towel and squeeze out all of the liquid. Make sure it is as dry as you can get it.
- Add the cauliflower, Parmesan cheese, Italian seasoning, garlic, salt, pepper and the egg to a large bowl. Mix together until the mixture holds together.
- Line the crisper cookie sheet with parchment paper and brush with olive oil.

- Spread the mixture onto the cookie sheet.
- Bake for 15 minutes until the crust is slightly golden.
- Now start prepping for your pizza creation.
- Choose from a combination of sauces in Section 9 pg. 40 (Recipes start on Page 41)
- Choose from our creative list of toppings in Section 10 (Starts on Page 72)

ZUCCHINI CRUST

Zucchini is great in spaghetti and even in place of noodles. But, who would have thought to make a crust out of it. This universal vegetable packs a crunch and a punch in your mouth that will have you use this ingredient for your crust anytime.

Total Time: 45 minutes

Makes: 6 Servings

INGREDIENTS:

2 cups shredded zucchini, dried

2 large eggs, lightly beaten

¼ cup all-purpose flour

¼ tsp. salt

1/4 cup Parmesan cheese

½ cup Mozzarella cheese

1 tbsp. olive oil

DIRECTIONS:

> Equipment needed: crisper cookie sheet, peel, parchment paper, and brush (for oil)
> Preheat oven to 475.
> Combine all ingredients into a large bowl
> Line the pizza peel with parchment paper and brush with olive oil.
> Spread the mixture onto the peel until if forms a 12-inch-wide circle.
> Place the parchment paper onto the cookie sheet.
> Bake for 15 minutes until the crust is slightly golden, then start prepping your pizza.
> Choose from a combination of sauces in Section 9 pg. 40 (Recipes start on Page 41)
> Choose from our creative list of toppings in Section 10 (Starts on Page 72)

BUTTERNUT SQUASH CRUST

This grain free pizza crust gives your pizza a sweet and creamy flavor that you cannot get with cauliflower. So, just pick your toppings and have fun with it.

Total Time: 67 minutes

Makes: 4 Servings

INGREDIENTS:

1 ½ cups butternut squash, mashed

½ cups all-purpose flour

½ cup shredded Mozzarella cheese

1 tbsp. Parmesan cheese

½ tsp. fresh sage, minced

½ tsp. baking powder

½ tsp. salt

¼ tsp. granulated garlic

1 pinch nutmeg

1 pinch cayenne pepper

1 egg, beaten

1 tbsp. olive oil

DIRECTIONS:

- Equipment needed: crisper cookie sheet, peel, parchment paper, and brush (for oil)
- Preheat oven to 475.
- Pour all of the ingredients into a large bowl.

Crisper Tray Pizza Recipe Cookbook

- Line the pizza peel with parchment paper and brush with olive oil.
- Spread the mixture onto the peel until if forms a 12-inch-wide circle.
- Place the parchment paper onto the cookie sheet.
- Bake for 25 minutes until the crust is slightly golden, flip and bake for 15 minutes more.
- Now start prepping for your pizza creation.
- Choose from a combination of sauces in Section 9 pg. 40 (Recipes start on Page 41)
- Choose from our creative list of toppings in Section 10 (Starts on Page 72)

WHOLE-WHEAT DOUGH

There tends to be a bad rap when it comes to whole-wheat anything. Sometimes it can be flavorless and tough. But, we guarantee that this recipe will have you wondering if you used regular flour instead.

Total Time: 15 minutes

Makes: 4 Servings

INGREDIENTS:

¾ cup whole-wheat flour

¾ cup all-purpose flour

1 package quick rising yeast

¾ tsp. salt

¼ tsp. sugar

2/3 cup hot water

2 tsp. extra-virgin olive oil

DIRECTIONS:

› Equipment needed: crisper tray, peel, and brush (for oil)

› Preheat oven to 475.

› Combine flour, yeast, salt and sugar in a food processor.

› Combine the hot water and oil in a measuring cup and gradually pour in the liquid while the mixture is pulsing.

› Sprinkle olive oil in a large bowl and coat the dough with the oil. Cover the dough with plastic wrap and set in a warm setting for no less than 1 ½ hrs.

› Punch the dough down to release the air.

› Sprinkle the peel with cornmeal.

- Flatten the dough on the peel to make a 12-inch-wide circle.
- Lift the dough to create a lip at the edges.
- Brush the top lightly with olive oil.
- With your fingers push dents into the surface to prevent bubbling.
- Now start prepping for your pizza creation.
- Choose from a combination of sauces in Section 9 pg. 40 (Recipes start on Page 41)
- Choose from our creative list of toppings in Section 10 (Starts on Page 72)

FLATBREAD (GLUTEN FREE) PIZZA CRUST

Flatbread gives the exotic feel to the pizza. It is soft, flaky, and can be cut into squares. But, above all, it is gluten free.

Total Time: 20 minutes

Makes: 8 Servings

INGREDIENTS:

Makes enough for two 10-12 inch pizzas

1 cup tapioca flour

½ cup coconut flour

¼ tsp. salt

½ cup canned coconut milk

¼ cup butter

¼ cup water

3 garlic cloves, minced

1 egg

DIRECTIONS:

- Equipment needed: Crisper cookie sheet and peel.
- Preheat oven to 475.
- Mix the tapioca and coconut flour and salt together in a medium bowl.
- Using a small pot, heat the coconut milk, butter, water and garlic over medium high until it simmers.
- Mix the hot and dry ingredients together.
- Let cool.

- Whisk the egg and add to the mixture.
- Let sit for 5 minutes.
- Sprinkle the cookie sheet with cornmeal.
- Spread the dough thinly on the cookie sheet to fit.
- Bake for 7 minutes.
- Now start prepping for your pizza creation.
- Choose from a combination of sauces in Section 9 pg. 40 (Recipes start on Page 41)
- Choose from our creative list of toppings in Section 10 (Starts on Page 72)

BEET STYLE PIZZA CRUST

Beets usually have a very strong flavor, but you cannot taste them in the crust. The best thing about the crust, besides it being good for you, is the fact that it is so colorfu . It can be great eye candy for your next event.

Total Time: 30 minutes

Makes: 8 Servings

INGREDIENTS:

Makes enough for two 10-12 inch pizzas

1 cup warm water

2 tsp dry active yeast

3 cups flour

2 tsp. salt

2 tsp. honey

¾ cup beet, cooked and pureed

DIRECTIONS:

> Equipment needed: Crisper tray, parchment paper
> Preheat oven to 475.
> Mix the water and yeast together.
> Add flour, honey, and beets to the mixture.
> Knead the dough on a countertop until it is mixed well.
> Form into a ball and oil a bowl. Place inside the bowl and cover with wrap.
> Let sit for 2 hours.

- Divide the dough into two separate crusts and can refrigerate one for later.
- Lay parchment paper on the countertop and sprinkle with cornmeal
- Spread the dough thinly on the parchment paper to fit into the shape of the crisper basket. Move around a little to make it fit if needed.
- Flip the dough over into the crisper tray so it fits evenly.
- Bake for 7 minutes.
- Now start prepping for your pizza creation.
- Choose from a combination of sauces in Section 9 pg. 40 (Recipes start on Page 41)
- Choose from our creative list of toppings in Section 10 (Starts on Page 72)

EGGPLANT PIZZA CRUST

This low-carb, earthy crust is going to make you love this pizza even more. Deliciousness is something we do not compromise here, just the carbs.

Total Time: 20 minutes

Makes: 3 Servings

INGREDIENTS:

1 large eggplant, cut into ¼ inch slices

1 ½ tsp. salt

6 oz. Parmesan Cheese

1 ½ tsp. extra-virgin olive oil

1 garlic clove, minced

DIRECTIONS:

- Equipment needed: crisper tray (enough for 2), parchment paper, brush (for oil)
- Preheat oven to 425.
- Line baking sheet with paper towels.
- Place each of the eggplant slices in one layer on baking sheet.
- Sprinkle each piece with salt and let sit for 15 minutes.
- Pat the eggplant dry.
- Brush oil onto your crisper and arrange the eggplant to fit into the crisper basket.
- Sprinkle with 1 cup Parmesan cheese.
- Cook for 15 minutes.
- Now start prepping for your pizza creation.
- Choose from a combination of sauces in Section 9 pg. 40 (Recipes start on Page 41)
- Choose from our creative list of toppings in Section 10 (Starts on Page 72)

SWEET POTATO PIZZA CRUST

Sweet potatoes are so versatile that we had to make a pizza crust out of them. When cooking the crust, you are going to love the color, the aroma of the spices and the puffiness of the crust. It is going to knock you out of this world.

Total Time: 50 minutes

Makes: 8 Servings

INGREDIENTS:

3 sweet potatoes, medium

1 cup almond flour

1 egg

½ tsp. salt

1 tsp. dried oregano

1 tsp. dried basil

1 tsp. garlic powder

1 tbsp. apple cider vinegar

DIRECTIONS:

- Equipment needed: Pizza Stone and peel
- Preheat oven to 400.
- Cook the potatoes in the microwave until soft.
- Peel and add to large mixing bowl with flour, egg, salt, dried oregano, basil, garlic powder and apple cider vinegar.
- Mash until combined.
- Mix the tapioca and coconut flour and salt together in a medium bowl.

- Using a small pot, heat the coconut milk, butter, water and garlic over medium high until it simmers. Sprinkle the crisper cookie sheet with cornmeal
- Spread the dough thinly on the crisper cookie sheet.
- Bake for 30 minutes.
- Now start prepping for your pizza creation.
- Choose from a combination of sauces in Section 9 pg. 40 (Recipes start on Page 41)
- Choose from our creative list of toppings in Section 10 (Starts on Page 72)

SECTION 9: COMBINATION OF SAUCES:

Let's get saucy everyone! We know that everyone loves pizza and the sauce can make or break the pizza. If you do not combine the right sauce with the correct toppings, your pizza is going to taste a little off. This particular section will help you decide what sauce goes great with the type of toppings you want to put on your pizza.

We have engineered a sauce recipe for everyone in this section. For those who are allergic to tomatoes, we have an alternative variety that will make your mouth water in ways you would have never imagined. The Savory Pumpkin Puree Sauce or No Tomatoes in this Tomato Sauce are made with pumpkin puree and beets, which give the sauce a great color, but your taste buds, will never know that you are not eating tomatoes at all.

This section also provides many different types of sauces for those who want to try something new. From creamy Alfredo to nutty pesto or from zesty salsa to Greek style hummus, this section has a type of sauce that everyone will enjoy.

PINE NUTTY PESTO SAUCE

Pesto sauce is the nutty alternative to tomato sauce. Spread it on your pizza dough and see what will go with its nutty flavor

Total Time: 15 minutes

Makes: 1 cup

INGREDIENTS:

2 cups fresh basil leaves

½ cup Parmesan cheese, grated

½ cup extra virgin olive oil

1/3 cup pine nuts

3 garlic cloves, minced

½ tsp. Salt

½ tsp. Pepper

DIRECTIONS:

- Equipment needed: Food processor
- Pour the basil and pine nuts in the food processor
- Pulse several times
- Next, add in the garlic and cheese.
- Pulse several times
- Scrape the sides with a spatula
- While running, stir in the olive oil
- Do not let it separate
- Stir in the salt and pepper to taste

- Now start prepping for your toppings.
- Choose from our creative list of toppings in Section 10 (Starts on Page 72)

CREAMY BECHAMEL SAUCE

If you're tired of the traditional pizza – Have no Fear! This white sauce will add a little creaminess to your pie.

Total Time: 15 minutes

Makes: 2 cups

INGREDIENTS:

¼ cup butter

1/3 cup flour, plain

2 cups milk

1 ¼ cheddar cheese, grated

3 tbsp. Parmesan cheese, grated

½ tsp. Nutmeg

½ tsp. Salt

½ tsp. Pepper

DIRECTIONS:

- Pour the butter in a saucepan and melt over low heat
- Next, add the flour and whisk until the mixture is smooth
- Cook for 2 minutes
- Gradually stir in the milk to avoid lumps
- Add the salt, pepper and nutmeg.
- Cook for 7 minutes. Remember to stir frequently to thicken the sauce.
- Remove when it comes to a boil.

- Stir in the cheese and
- Now start prepping for your toppings.
- Choose from our creative list of toppings in Section 10 (Starts on Page 72)

ZESTY SALSA RECIPE

Salsa is one of the most universal foods I know. Is it an appetizer? Is it a sauce? We'll let you be the judge.

Total Time: 10 minutes

Makes: 2 cups

INGREDIENTS:

1 medium lime, juice

10 Roma tomatoes

½ cup cilantro, fresh

1 garlic clove

¼ of a medium red onion, chopped

1 jalapeno

1 tbsp. olive oil

½ tsp. Salt

DIRECTIONS:

- Equipment needed: food processor
- Pour all of the ingredients into a food processor. Pulse until well mixed, but chunky.
- Salt to taste
- For a thicker sauce, strain some of the liquid.
- Pour enough sauce over the dough to cover dough/crust and spread all around.
- Now start prepping for your toppings.
- Choose from our creative list of toppings in Section 10 (Starts on Page 72)

SWEET AND TANGY BARBEQUE SAUCE

Barbeque sauce is great slathered on anything. Why would your pizza be any different? Combine the two together and you will not be disappointed.

Total Time: 25 minutes

Makes: 2 cups

INGREDIENTS:

1 tbsp. olive oil

½ small onion, chopped

1 garlic clove, chopped

1 cup ketchup

¼ cup apple cider vinegar

¼ cup molasses

2 tbsp. brown sugar

2 tbsp. Dijon mustard

2 tsp. Worcestershire sauce

1 tbsp. chili powder

¼ tsp. cayenne pepper

¾ cup water

½ tsp. Salt

½ tsp. Pepper

DIRECTIONS:

> Pour the oil in a medium saucepan and heat.
> Add in the onion, and garlic.
> Cook for 5 minutes and stir frequently.

- Next, add the rest of the ingredients and let simmer for 15 minutes until it thickens.
- Sir frequently
- Pour enough sauce over the dough to cover dough/crust and spread all around.
- Now start prepping for your toppings.
- Choose from our creative list of toppings in Section 10 (Starts on Page 72)

SAVORY PUMPKIN PUREE SAUCE

Pumpkin on a pizza? This is a great alternative for those who can't eat tomatoes because of their acidity. Try this sauce and you won't even notice the difference.

Total Time: 15 minutes

Makes: 2 cups

INGREDIENTS:

2 cups pumpkin puree

2 cup tomato sauce

1 garlic cloves, minced

1 tsp. Italian seasoning

DIRECTIONS:

- Mix all of the ingredients in a saucepan.
- Simmer for 15 minutes on medium heat.
- Stir frequently.
- Add more seasoning if desired.
- Pour enough sauce over the dough to cover dough/crust and spread all around.
- Now start prepping for your toppings.
- Choose from our creative list of toppings in Section 10 (Starts on Page 72)

HUM FOR HUMMUS STYLE PIZZA SAUCE

Hummus – the Greek Salsa – is a great healthy way to jazz up your pizza. Add some onion, peppers, olives and feta cheese to your pizza.

Total Time: 5 minutes

Makes: 3 cups

INGREDIENTS:

2/3 cup of tahini, roasted

¼ cup extra virgin olive oil

2 garlic cloves, mashed

1 25-oz cans of garbanzo beans, drained

¼ cup lemon juice, freshly squeezed

½ cup water

½ cup salt

Garnish: paprika, olive oil, toasted pine nuts, chopped parsley

DIRECTIONS:

- Equipment needed: Food Processor
- Pour the tahini and olive oil in a food processor and pulse smoothly.
- Add the garlic, garbanzo beans, lemon juice, water and salt in the food processor.
- Mix until smooth.
- Add more salt and lemon juice to taste.
- Pour enough sauce over the dough to cover dough/crust and spread all around.
- Now start prepping for your toppings.
- Choose from our creative list of toppings in Section 10 (Starts on Page 72)

NO TOMATO IN THIS TOMATO SAUCE

Combining beets and pumpkin together makes for a great sauce. The beets are both sweet and add a great color to the sauce. Pair some garlic and basil and you will love this change to the norm.

Total Time: 45 minutes

Makes: 4 cups

INGREDIENTS:

3 tbsp. olive oil

1 medium red onion, chopped

½ tsp. thyme, dried

5 garlic cloves, minced

1 ½ cup carrots, sliced into coins

3 tbsp. lemon juice, freshly squeezed

1 tbsp. balsamic vinegar

2 cups pumpkin puree

1 package peeled and ready to eat beets

½ tsp. Salt

½ tsp. Pepper

DIRECTIONS:

- Pour the olive oil in a skillet and heat.
- Sauté the onion and thyme for 10 minutes. Stir often.
- Add the garlic and sauté for 1 minute
- Next, add the carrots, lemon juice, balsamic vinegar, salt and pepper and water to cover the carrots

- Let the ingredients come to a boil.
- Lower the heat, cover and simmer for 30 minutes
- While the carrots are cooking, add the beets and the pumpkin puree to a blender.
- Mix until smooth
- When carrots are done cooking, scoop into the blender and blend with the pumpkin mixture.
- Pour enough sauce over the dough to cover dough/crust and spread all around.
- Now start prepping for your toppings.
- Choose from our creative list of toppings in Section 10 (Starts on Page 72)

BLACK OLIVE TAPENADE SAUCE

Olives and pizza go together like peanut butter and jelly. Spread it thickly on your dough, with some grilled vegetables.

Total Time: 6 minutes

Makes: 1 cup

INGREDIENTS:

7 oz. black olives, pitted

1 garlic clove, minced

3 anchovies

8 small capers

2 tbsp. olive oil, divided

DIRECTIONS:

- Equipment needed: Food Processor
- Pour olives, garlic, anchovies, capers and 1 tbsp. olive oil in the food processor
- Mix for 15 seconds
- Scrape down the edges with a spatula
- Add the other tbsp. of olive oil
- Process for 30 seconds until smooth.
- Make sure there are no garlic chunks left
- Pour enough sauce over the dough to cover dough/crust and spread all around.
- Now start prepping for your toppings.
- Choose from our creative list of toppings in Section 10 (Starts on Page 72)

CARROT CHILI PASTE SAUCE

A North African chili paste will show you a whole new way to eat pizza. Let us start thinking outside the box.

Total Time: 20 minutes

Makes: 3 1/2 cups

INGREDIENTS:

2 cups vegetable broth

1 lb. carrots, peeled and coarsely chopped

2 medium garlic cloves

1 15 oz. can garbanzo beans, drained

4 tbsp. extra virgin olive oil

3 tbsp. almond butter

5 large ice cubes

4 tbsp. harissa paste

2 tbsp. lemon juiced, freshly squeezed

1 tbsp. honey

½ tsp. Salt

½ tsp. Pepper

DIRECTIONS:

- Pour the vegetable broth in a small saucepan.
- Bring to boil over high heat.
- Next, add the garlic and carrots.
- Reduce to medium and cook for 10 minutes,

- Remove from the stove and let cool.
- Place the carrots, garlic, 1 ½ cups cooking liquid and the garbanzo beans in a food processor
- Mix until smooth.
- Add the olive oil, almond butter and ice cubes with the mixture.
- Pulse until smooth
- Mix in 3 tbsp. of the harissa, lemon juice, honey, salt and pepper and pulse.
- Taste and add more seasoning as desired.
- Pour enough sauce over the dough to cover dough/crust and spread all around.
- Now start prepping for your toppings.
- Choose from our creative list of toppings in Section 10 (Starts on Page 72)

GARLIC AND OLIVE OIL SAUCE

When you are mincing up the garlic, remember not to overdo it. Rub this sauce on your dough and then add some light toppings for a more refined type of pizza pie.

Total Time: 5 minutes

Makes: 2 cups

INGREDIENTS:

½ cup extra virgin olive oil

6 large garlic cloves, peeled

¼ cup parsley leaves, minced

¼ tsp Salt

½ tsp. Pepper

DIRECTIONS:

> Pour first four ingredients into a small skillet
> Cook for 5 minutes on medium-low
> Stir often
> Remove from the stove
> Stir in parsley and pepper
> Pour enough sauce over the dough to cover dough/crust and spread all around.
> Now start prepping for your toppings.
> Choose from our creative list of toppings in Section 10 (Starts on Page 72)

PEPPERY JELLY PIZZA STYLE SAUCE

If you're tired of the traditional cheese pizza – Try pepper jelly. This will give your pizza a unique flavor that you will run to every time you want to eat something out of the norm.

Total Time: 15 minutes

Makes: 2 cups

INGREDIENTS:

1 jar Smucker's apple jelly

5 medium jalapenos, chopped

1 tsp. red pepper flakes

½ tsp. garlic powder

½ tsp. tabasco

½ tsp. black pepper

DIRECTIONS:

> Pour the jelly in a saucepan and warm over low heat
> Make sure that it becomes a liquid like consistency
> Mix in the other ingredients and mix well
> Put ingredients back in the jar
> Put in fridge
> Take out every 30 minutes and shake until peppers evenly distribute throughout the jelly
> Pour enough sauce over the dough to cover dough/crust and spread all around. Now start prepping for your toppings.
> Choose from our creative list of toppings in Section 10 (Starts on Page 72)

MISO AND MACADAMIAN NUT RICOTTA SAUCE

Ricotta cheese is the cream cheese of Italian cuisine. When creating your pie, spread a thin layer and even add basil, grilled vegetables, tomatoes and even lemon to give you pizza a taste to remember.

Total Time: 5 minutes

Makes: 2 cups

INGREDIENTS:

1 ½ cups macadamia nuts

3 tbsp. lemon juice

1 tbsp. nutritional yeast

1 tbsp. white miso paste

1 garlic clove

¼ cup water

DIRECTIONS:

> Equipment needed: food processor
> Pour the macadamia nuts, lemon juice, yeast, miso paste, garlic and water into the food processor
> Blend until smooth and has a creamy texture
> Scrape down the sides with a spatula.
> Add 1 tsp. of water if needed until the ricotta texture is reached
> Pour enough sauce over the dough to cover dough/crust and spread all around.
> Now start prepping for your toppings.
> Choose from our creative list of toppings in Section 10 (Starts on Page 72)

CARAMELIZED ONION SAUCE

Caramelized onions are a savory treat. When topping your pizza remember to compliment the sauce with some feta cheese, mushrooms, arugula, prosciutto and balsamic vinegar.

Total Time: 35 minutes

Makes: 2 cups

INGREDIENTS:

1 tbsp. butter

3 cups onion, thinly sliced

1 cup red wine, dry

3 cups low sodium chicken broth

1/8 tsp. salt

1/8 tsp. black pepper

DIRECTIONS:

- Pour the butter into a large skillet and melt over medium heat
- Mix in the onion
- Cook for 5 minutes and stir frequently
- Continue to cook for 15 minutes
- Add the wine and cook for 5 more minutes
- Remove the onion from the pan and finely chop
- Return to pan
- Add in the broth, salt and pepper and stir

- Let it come to a boil
- And cook for 10 minutes until it is reduced to 2 cups
- Pour enough sauce over the dough to cover dough/crust and spread all around.
- Now start prepping for your toppings.
- Choose from our creative list of toppings in Section 10 (Starts on Page 72)

GO BACK TO THE BASICS TOMATO SAUCE

There is nothing wrong with going back to the basics and spreading your pie with tomato sauce. Sometimes it's good to go back to what made us fall in love with pizza in the first place.

Total Time: 15 minutes

Makes: 2 cups

INGREDIENTS:

1 tbsp. olive oil

2 garlic cloves, minced

¼ cup red wine

1 28- oz. can crushed tomatoes

1 small can tomato paste

1 tbsp. sugar

1 tsp. Italian seasoning

½ tsp. Salt

½ tsp. Pepper

DIRECTIONS:

> Pour the oil in a medium saucepan
> Add the garlic
> Sauté over high heat for 1 minute
> Pour in the wine and simmer for 2 minutes
> Add the remaining ingredients and heat through.
> Taste and add seasonings if needed

- Pour enough sauce over the dough to cover dough/crust and spread all around.
- Now start prepping for your toppings.
- Choose from our creative list of toppings in Section 10 (Starts on Page 72)

MIDDLE EASTERN ZAATAR SAUCE

This Middle Eastern sauce makes for a great alternative for what you are used to. Pair it with tomatoes, feta, olives and even mint. See how that tastes on your palate.

Total Time: 8 minutes

Makes: 2 cups

INGREDIENTS:

3 tbsp. sesame seeds

3 tbsp. thyme leaves, thyme

1 tbsp. sumac powder

2/3 tsp. salt

DIRECTIONS:

- Pour the sesame seeds in dry skillet over medium heat
- Toast for 5 minutes
- Next, combine the seeds, thyme leaves, sumac and salt in a bowl
- Stir well
- Pour enough sauce over the dough to cover dough/crust and spread all around.
- Now start prepping for your toppings.
- Choose from our creative list of toppings in Section 10 (Starts on Page 72)

THAI PEANUT SAUCE

Turn your pizza into a Thai dish. By adding bean sprouts, scallions, chicken, anc ginger over your sauce you will have created a successful Thai-themed pizza.

Total Time: 8 minutes

Makes: 2 cups

INGREDIENTS:

1 14 oz. can coconut milk

3 tbsp. red curry paste

1 cup natural creamy peanut butter, unsweetened

3 tbsp. low sodium soy sauce

¼ cup honey

2 tbsp. rice vinegar

½ cup water

½ tsp. sesame oil

DIRECTIONS:

- Pour all the ingredients in a saucepan and bring to a simmer.
- Cook for 3 minutes
- Stir often
- Let the sauce cool.
- Pour enough sauce over the dough to cover dough/crust and spread all around.
- Now start prepping for your toppings.
- Choose from our creative list of toppings in Section 10 (Starts on Page 72)

JAPANESE LIME WASABI SAUCE

For those who want to try something different and spicy, this is the sauce for you. Add some ahi tuna or some crab meat and avocado with a sprinkle of soy sauce and you will have a sushi-themed pizza.

Total Time: 10 minutes

Makes: 1 cup

INGREDIENTS:

2 tbsp. lime juice, fresh

2 tbsp. wasabi sauce

1 tbsp. fresh ginger, minced

1 tbsp. rice vinegar

¼ tsp. salt

1/8 tsp. black pepper

½ cup olive oil

DIRECTIONS:

> Pour first six ingredients into a small bowl
> Stir in the olive oil
> Let rest
> Pour enough sauce over the dough to cover dough/crust and spread all around.
> Now start prepping for your toppings.
> Choose from our creative list of toppings in Section 10 (Starts on Page 72)

GARLIC AIOLI PIZZA SAUCE

Garlic Aioli is great paired with seafood and vegetables. Make a shrimp or tuna topped pizza with tomatoes and basil. You will have yourself a hit.

Total Time: 65 minutes

Makes: 2 cups

INGREDIENTS:

1 cup mayonnaise

3 garlic cloves, minced

1 tbsp. lemon juice

1 pinch cayenne pepper

DIRECTIONS:

> Pour all of the ingredients into a small bowl
> Stir together
> Cover with plastic wrap
> Refrigerate for 1 hour
> Pour enough sauce over the dough to cover dough/crust and spread all around.
> Now start prepping for your toppings.
> Choose from our creative list of toppings in Section 10 (Starts on Page 72)

BASIL AND SUN-DRIED TOMATO SAUCE

This is a sauce that will pair well with pepperoni and olive pizza. The flavors pack a punch that is simple, which is what we want from our ingredients.

Total Time: 20 minutes

Makes: 2 cups

INGREDIENTS:

2 tbsp. extra virgin olive oil

1 whole yellow onion, diced

3 garlic cloves, minced

3 whole sun-dried tomatoes packed in oil, drained and chopped

½ cup white wine, dry

1 can fire roasted tomatoes

1 can tomato sauce

1 tbsp. oregano, dried

2 tbsp. fresh basil, chopped

½ tsp. Salt

½ tsp. Pepper

DIRECTIONS:

- Pour the oil in a medium saucepan
- Heat over medium heat
- Add in the onion and sauté for 5 minutes
- Next, add in the garlic and sun-dried tomatoes
- Sauté for 2 minutes

- Remember not to burn the garlic
- Deglaze the pan with wine
- Simmer for 2 minutes
- Stir in tomatoes and tomato sauce
- Reduce the heat to medium low
- Stir in the oregano and basil
- Season with salt and pepper
- Simmer for 15 minutes to thicken sauce
- Pour enough sauce over the dough to cover dough/crust and spread all around.
- Now start prepping for your toppings.
- Choose from our creative list of toppings in Section 10 (Starts on Page 72)

LOWER IN FAT ALFREDO SAUCE

This sauce is similar to béchamel, but it is way creamier and cheesier. For those who love cheese, this is the great sauce for them.

Total Time: 15 minutes

Makes: 2 cups

INGREDIENTS:

¼ cup butter

¼ cup all-purpose flour

½ tsp. garlic salt

2 cup half and half

2 garlic cloves, minced

1 tbsp. parsley flakes, dried

1/3 cup Parmesan cheese, grated

DIRECTIONS:

- Pour the butter in a saucepan
- Melt the butter over medium heat
- Stir in the flour and garlic salt and mix smoothly
- Gradually beat the half and half in the sauce
- Stir in the garlic, parsley and Parmesan cheese
- Continue to stir
- Bring the sauce to a simmer and cook for 5 minutes
- Make sure the sauce has thickened
- Pour enough sauce over the dough to cover dough/crust and spread all around.

- Now start prepping for your toppings.
- Choose from our creative list of toppings in Section 10 (Starts on Page 72)

FIERY SPANISH ROMESCO SAUCE

This is one of those sauces that pairs with almost anything. Don't feel like you can't be creative here. Toss some chicken, shrimp, steak and vegetables on your pie and you will wonder why you didn't switch your sauce earlier.

Total Time: 5 minutes

Makes: 1 cup

INGREDIENTS:

1 7-oz. jar roasted red peppers, drained

1 slice sandwich bread, lightly toasted

¼ cup silvered almonds, toasted

1 tsp. Sherry vinegar

1 garlic clove

1 tbsp. olive oil

1 small jalapeno pepper, seeded

¼ tsp. ancho chili powder

½ tsp. paprika

½ tsp. kosher salt

DIRECTIONS:

> Equipment needed: Food processor
> Toast the silvered almonds at 350 for 3 minutes
> Pour all of the ingredients into the food processor
> Blend smoothly
> Taste and adjust the seasonings as needed
> Pour enough sauce over the dough to cover dough/crust and spread all around.

- Now start prepping for your toppings.
- Choose from our creative list of toppings in Section 10 (Starts on Page 72)

SECTION 10:
PIZZA TOPPINGS / LET'S GET CREATIVE:

Note: Cook time for your pizzas will be around 12-14 minutes. Depending on the type of oven you have this will vary, so just look for the cheese to melt and the crust to be browned.

THE ORIGINAL NEOPOLITAN

This pizza is known as the pizza that left Italy and made it to America. It is the pie that made Americans crazy for pizza and you and your family will not be disappointed.

RECCOMENDED:

RISING PIZZA DOUGH – REFER TO PAGE 29 OF PIZZA CRUST SECTION OR CHOOSE THE CRUST OF YOUR CHOICE

GARLIC AND OLIVE OIL SAUCE – REFER TO PAGE 56 OF PIZZA SAUCE SECTION OR CHOOSE THE CRUST OF YOUR CHOICE

TOPPINGS:

12 oz. buffalo mozzarella

6 tbsp. extra virgin olive oil

24 basil leaves

Salt, to taste

COOKING TIME:
Cooks 12-14 min.

Depending on the type of oven you have this will vary so just look for the cheese to melt and the crust to be browned.

SUNNY CALIFORNIA STYLE

The sun is always shining in California. At least that is what they say. Why should your pizza be any different? This Sunny California Style pizza will definitely brighten up your day.

RECCOMENDED:

CALIFLOWER CRUST – REFER TO PAGE 36 OF PIZZA CRUST SECTION OR CHOOSE THE CRUST OF YOUR CHOICE

SAVORY PUMPKIN PUREE SAUCE – REFER TO PAGE 49 OF PIZZA SAUCE SECTION OR CHOOSE THE CRUST OF YOUR CHOICE

TOPPINGS:

1 ½ cups Monterey Jack Cheese, shredded

2 cups cooked chicken, cut up

½ cup sliced ripe olives

1 medium avocado, sliced

1 fresh lemon, juice

COOKING TIME:

Cooks 12-14 min.

Depending on the type of oven you have this will vary so just look for the cheese to melt and the crust to be browned.

CHICAGO – THIN CRUST STYLE

The taste of Chicago Style Pizza on a thin crust! Something you can make at home on your very own pizza stone. You won't have to take any trips to Chicago to taste this masterpiece.

RECCOMENDED:

THIN CRUST – REFER TO PAGE 31 OF PIZZA CRUST SECTION OR CHOOSE THE CRUST OF YOUR CHOICE

PINE NUTTY PESTO SAUCE – REFER TO PAGE 45 OF PIZZA SAUCE SECTION OR CHOOSE THE CRUST OF YOUR CHOICE

TOPPINGS:

¾ cups mozzarella cheese, shredded

¾ cups cheddar, shredded

1 cup fennel- laced Italian Sausage

1 cup Italian beef

1 cup pepperoni

½ cup pepperchini's

Parmesan, shredded to taste

Romano, shredded to taste

COOKING TIME:

Cooks 12-14 min.

Depending on the type of oven you have this will vary so just look for the cheese to melt and the crust to be browned.

GREEK STYLE PIZZA

Greece is full of many incredible ingredients. The freshness and brightness of the ingredients makes you feel like you are relaxing by the Mediterranean Sea.

RECCOMENDED:

WHOLE WEAT DOUGH – REFER TO PAGE 39 OF PIZZA CRUST SECTION OR CHOOSE THE CRUST OF YOUR CHOICE

HUM FOR HUMMUS STYLE PIZZA SAUCE – REFER TO PAGE 50 OF PIZZA SAUCE SECTION OR CHOOSE THE CRUST OF YOUR CHOICE

TOPPINGS:

1 cup cooked lamb, cut into strips

1 red onion, sliced

4 oz. fresh spinach, roughly chopped

2 red pepper halves, roughly chopped

¾ cup Kalamata olives, halved

6 oz. feta cheese, crumbled

COOKING TIME:

Cooks 12-14 min.

Depending on the type of oven you have this will vary so just look for the cheese to melt and the crust to be browned.

ST. LOUIS STYLE

This pizza is so close to New York Style pizza, except for the crust. This super thin yeast-less crust is cut in squares and piled high with some of your favorite cheeses and toppings.

RECCOMENDED:

ST. LOUIS STYLE PIZZA CRUST - REFER TO PAGE 34 OF PIZZA CRUST SECTION OR CHOOSE THE CRUST OF YOUR CHOICE

NO TOMATO IN THIS TOMATO SAUCE - REFER TO PAGE 51 OF PIZZA SAUCE SECTION OR CHOOSE THE CRUST OF YOUR CHOICE

TOPPINGS:

1 cup white cheddar cheese, shredded

½ cup Swiss cheese, shredded

½ cup provolone cheese, shredded

1 tsp. liquid hickory liquid smoke

2 tsp. oregano

2 tsp. basil

1 tsp. thyme

½ red onion

½ green pepper

½ cup sausage

½ cup cooked hamburger meat

½ cup pepperoni

½ cup bacon

¾ cup mushrooms

½ cup black olives

¼ cup anchovy

½ cup Canadian bacon

¼ cup jalapenos

½ cup pineapples

½ cup banana peppers

½ cup tomatoes

COOKING TIME:
Cooks 12-14 min.

Depending on the type of oven you have this will vary so just look for the cheese to melt and the crust to be browned.

THAI CHICKEN STYLE PIZZA

The sweet and spicy flavors of Thai cuisine pair well with any type of dough: whether in a sandwich or on pizza dough. The crunchiness of the peanuts with the bean sprouts will give you a different definition of pizza.

RECCOMENDED:

BEET STYLE PIZZA CRUST - REFER TO PAGE 41 OF PIZZA CRUST SECTION OR CHOOSE THE CRUST OF YOUR CHOICE

THAI PEANUT SAUCE - REFER TO PAGE 62 OF PIZZA SAUCE SECTION OR CHOOSE THE CRUST OF YOUR CHOICE

TOPPINGS:

1 tbsp. olive oil

2 chicken breasts cut into cubes

2 cups mozzarella cheese, shredded

4 green onions, slivered diagonally

½ cup bean sprouts

1/3 cup shredded carrot

2 tbsp. roasted peanuts, chopped

2 tbsp. fresh cilantro, chopped

COOKING TIME:

Cooks 12-14 min.

Depending on the type of oven you have this will vary so just look for the cheese to melt and the crust to be browned.

MEXICAN STYLE PIZZA

The zesty taste of salsa smothered on dough, and topped with beans, avocado and sour cream gives you the illusion of eating a chewy, savory taco.

RECCOMENDED:

CRACKER PIZZA CRUST – REFER TO PAGE 33 OF PIZZA CRUST SECTION OR CHOOSE THE CRUST OF YOUR CHOICE

ZESTY SALSA RECIPE – REFER TO PAGE 47 OF PIZZA SAUCE SECTION OR CHOOSE THE CRUST OF YOUR CHOICE

TOPPINGS:

1 16 oz. can refried beans

1 lb. ground beef

1 package taco seasoning mix

2 cups cheddar cheese, shredded

8 tbsp. sour cream

2 Roma tomatoes, chopped

2 green onions, chopped

1 4 oz. can diced green chilies, drained

½ avocado, diced

1 tbsp. black olives, sliced

COOKING TIME:

Cooks 12-14 min.

Depending on the type of oven you have this will vary so just look for the cheese to melt and the crust to be browned.

NEW ORLEANS MUFFALETTA STYLE PIZZA

This pizza combines all the flavors of the famous sandwich on top of dough. The toppings include lots of meat, olives, cheese, peppers and garlic. This is one hearty and delicious pizza.

RECCOMENDED:

ZUCCHINI CRUST – REFER TO PAGE 37 OF PIZZA CRUST SECTION OR CHOOSE THE CRUST OF YOUR CHOICE

BLACK OLIVE TAPENADE SAUCE – REFER TO PAGE 53 OF PIZZA SAUCE SECTION OR CHOOSE THE CRUST OF YOUR CHOICE

TOPPINGS:

Olive salad

½ cup mixed chopped olives

¼ cup chopped roasted red peppers

¼ cup chopped marinated artichoke hearts

2 tbsp. olive oil

1 tbsp. red wine vinegar

2 garlic cloves, minced

¼ tsp. red pepper flakes

¼ tsp. dried oregano

Other toppings

½ cup shredded mozzarella

3 slices provolone cheese, cut into strips

3 slices salami, cut into strips

3 slices Mortadella, cut into strips

3 slices Capicolla Prosciutto, cut into strips

COOKING TIME:
Cooks 12-14 min.

Depending on the type of oven you have this will vary so just look for the cheese to melt and the crust to be browned.

HAWAIIAN STYLE PIZZA

Everyone loves Hawaiian Barbeque. How about tossing some of that Kalua pork and green onions on your pie? You will fill like you are watching the Hawaiian sunset when you bite into this masterpiece.

RECCOMENDED:

RISING PIZZA DOUGH – REFER TO PAGE 29 OF PIZZA CRUST SECTION OR CHOOSE THE CRUST OF YOUR CHOICE

SWEET AND TANGY BARBEQUE SAUCE – REFER TO PAGE 48 OF PIZZA SAUCE SECTION OR CHOOSE THE CRUST OF YOUR CHOICE

TOPPINGS:

2 cups Kalua Pork

3 oz. Fontina, grated

1 oz. Parmesan, grated

1 ½ cup mozzarella cheese, shredded

6 strips bacon, diced

1 20 oz. can pineapple chunks, drained

½ cup bell pepper, thinly sliced

¼ cup green onion, sliced

¼ cup red onion, diced

2 tbsp. cilantro, chopped

COOKING TIME:
Cooks 12-14 min.

Depending on the type of oven you have this will vary so just look for the cheese to melt and the crust to be browned.

PISSALADIERE FRENCH STYLE PIZZA

This pizza will pair well with a thin crust and the caramelized onion sauce. The ingredients on this pie will melt in your mouth and having you explore different types of pizza.

RECCOMENDED:

THIN CRUST – REFER TO PAGE 31 OF PIZZA CRUST SECTION OR CHOOSE THE CRUST OF YOUR CHOICE

CARMELIZED ONION SAUCE – REFER TO PAGE 59 OF PIZZA SAUCE SECTION OR CHOOSE THE CRUST OF YOUR CHOICE

TOPPINGS:

1 ½ large onions, sliced

3 anchovy filets, chopped

1 garlic clove, minced

6 Kalamata, green and black olives, halved and pitted

Thyme, for garnish

COOKING TIME:

Cooks 12-14 min.

Depending on the type of oven you have this will vary so just look for the cheese to melt and the crust to be browned.

SALAD SYTLE PIZZA

The taste of summer in your mouth! This tangy Italian chopped salad will provide a freshness that you never thought would go on top of any pie.

SUGGESTED CRUST AND SAUCE:

FLATBREAD PIZZA CRUST – REFER TO PAGE 40 OF PIZZA CRUST SECTION OR CHOOSE THE CRUST OF YOUR CHOICE

GARLIC AIOLI PIZZA SAUCE – REFER TO PAGE 56 OF PIZZA SAUCE SECTION OR CHOOSE THE CRUST OF YOUR CHOICE

TOPPINGS:

2 cups mozzarella cheese

1 cup romaine lettuce, shredded

½ cup chickpeas

6 cherry tomatoes, sliced

3 slices of salami, stripped

4 pepperoncini, diced

¼ olives, chopped

Parsley, to taste

Basil, to taste

Feta cheese, to taste

Parmesan, to taste

COOKING TIME:
Cooks 12-14 min.

Depending on the type of oven you have this will vary so just look for the cheese to melt and the crust to be browned.

Leona Stellenberg

MIAMI-CUBAN STYLE PIZZA

The taste of Miami on a pie! The crunchiness of the corn, mixed with the beans, and cheese leaves for a nice, healthy and hearty meal.

SUGGESTED CRUST AND SAUCE:

EGGPLANT PIZZA CRUST – REFER TO PAGE 42 OF PIZZA CRUST SECTION OR CHOOSE THE CRUST OF YOUR CHOICE

MIDDLE EASTERN ZAATAR SAUCE – REFER TO PAGE 61 OF PIZZA SAUCE SECTION OR CHOOSE THE CRUST OF YOUR CHOICE

TOPPINGS:

1 110-oz can whole-kernel corn, drained

½ tsp. cumin seeds

1 cups roasted chicken breast, diced

1 15-oz. can black beans, rinsed and drained

1 garlic clove, minced

2 tbsp. fresh lemon juice

¾ cup Monterey Jack cheese with jalapeno peppers

4 tsp. fresh cilantro, chopped

COOKING TIME:

Cooks 12-14 min.

Depending on the type of oven you have this will vary so just look for the cheese to melt and the crust to be browned.

GERMAN SAUSAGE PIZZA

German is known for their beer and for their bratwurst. Two ingredients that you would never think would go with pizza. Well in this pie, we mix apricot preserves, with sauerkraut and bratwurst. Let us know what you think.

SUGGESTED CRUST AND SAUCE:

SWEET POTATO PIZZA CRUST – REFER TO PAGE 43 OF PIZZA CRUST SECTION OR CHOOSE THE CRUST OF YOUR CHOICE

BASIL AND SUN-DRIED TOMATO SAUCE – REFER TO PAGE 65 OF PIZZA SAUCE SECTION OR CHOOSE THE CRUST OF YOUR CHOICE

TOPPINGS:

1/3 cup apricot preserves

8 oz. uncooked bratwurst links, casings removed

1 large onion, chopped

1 cup sauerkraut, drained

1 ½ cup Monterey Jack cheese, shredded

COOKING TIME:

Cooks 12-14 min.

Depending on the type of oven you have this will vary so just look for the cheese to melt and the crust to be browned.

WHITE CLAM STYLE PIZZA

If you want to try something different then try this pizza. With a thin crust, and a creamy Alfredo sauce. This pie will be one of the most appealing things you have ever tasted.

SUGGESTED CRUST AND SAUCE:

RISING DOUGH PIZZA CRUST – REFER TO PAGE 29 OF PIZZA CRUST SECTION OR CHOOSE THE CRUST OF YOUR CHOICE

CREAMY BECHAMEL SAUCE – REFER TO PAGE 46 OF PIZZA SAUCE SECTION OR CHOOSE THE CRUST OF YOUR CHOICE

TOPPINGS:

24 littleneck clams, scrubbed, shucked

1 wedge Pecorino-Romano cheese

1 handful of fresh oregano

4 garlic cloves, sliced

Extra virgin olive oil, to taste

COOKING TIME:
Cooks 12-14 min.

Depending on the type of oven you have this will vary so just look for the cheese to melt and the crust to be browned.

BREAKFAST STYLE PIZZA

This pizza is something you can eat any time of the day. Scrambled eggs, sausage and hash browns go great on high rising dough.

SUGGESTED CRUST AND SAUCE:

FLATBREAD PIZZA CRUST – REFER TO PAGE 40 OF PIZZA CRUST SECTION OR CHOOSE THE CRUST OF YOUR CHOICE

FIERY SPANISH ROMESCO SAUCE – REFER TO PAGE 68 OF PIZZA SAUCE SECTION OR CHOOSE THE CRUST OF YOUR CHOICE

TOPPINGS:

6 eggs, scrambled

1 lb. ground breakfast sausage

1 cup frozen hash browns, thawed

1 package bacon bits

1 cup Monterey Jack cheese, shredded

1 cup cheddar cheese, shredded

COOKING TIME:

Cooks 12-14 min.

Depending on the type of oven you have this will vary so just look for the cheese to melt and the crust to be browned.

CHICKEN ALFREDO STYLE PIZZA

A classic Italian favorite dish can now be found on top of a pizza crust. The gooiness of the cheese, the creaminess of the Alfredo sauce, mixed with the spinach and tomatoes will pop in your mouth.

SUGGESTED CRUST AND SAUCE:

THIN CRUST – REFER TO PAGE 31 OF PIZZA CRUST SECTION OR CHOOSE THE CRUST OF YOUR CHOICE

LOWER IN FAT ALFREDO SAUCE – REFER TO PAGE 67 OF PIZZA SAUCE SECTION OR CHOOSE THE CRUST OF YOUR CHOICE

TOPPINGS:

1 garlic clove, minced

1 tsp. red pepper flakes

¼ cup Parmesan, grated

2 cups baby spinach, well washed and dried

1 cup grape tomatoes, red and yellow

1 cup mozzarella, grated

1 boneless skinless chicken breast, cubed

Salt, to taste

Pepper, to taste

COOKING TIME:

Cooks 12-14 min.

Depending on the type of oven you have this will vary so just look for the cheese to melt and the crust to be browned.

MEAT LOVERS STYLE PIZZA

Can't decide on what type of meat to put on your pie! Don't worry about it. This is your chance to top your pizza with all of the meat that you want.

SUGGESTED CRUST AND SAUCE:

HIGH RISING DOUGH – REFER TO PAGE 29 OF PIZZA CRUST SECTION OR CHOOSE THE CRUST OF YOUR CHOICE

GO BACK TO THE BASICS TOMATO SAUCE – REFER TO PAGE 60 OF PIZZA SAUCE SECTION OR CHOOSE THE CRUST OF YOUR CHOICE

TOPPINGS:

1/2 lb. lean ground beef

½ lb. bulk Italian sausage

½ cup pepperoni, sliced

1 oz. thinly sliced deli salami, cut into quarters

½ cup Canadian bacon, diced

1 cup cheddar cheese, shredded

1 cup mozzarella cheese, shredded

COOKING TIME:

Cooks 12-14 min.

Depending on the type of oven you have this will vary so just look for the cheese to melt and the crust to be browned.

VEGGIE STYLE PIZZA

There are some days when the idea of meat doesn't sound appealing. Or maybe you don't meat at all. Whatever the reason, this pie will satisfy all of your veggie craving needs.

SUGGESTED CRUST AND SAUCE:

THIN CRUST – REFER TO PAGE 31 OF PIZZA CRUST SECTION OR CHOOSE THE CRUST OF YOUR CHOICE

PEPPERY JELLY PIZZA SAUCE – REFER TO PAGE 57 OF PIZZA SAUCE SECTION OR CHOOSE THE CRUST OF YOUR CHOICE

TOPPINGS:

½ small onion, chopped

1 15-oz can tomatoes, diced

1 garlic clove, finely chopped

1 ¼ cup mozzarella cheese, shredded

½ cup green bell pepper, chopped

1.2 cup fresh mushrooms, sliced

¼ cup cheddar cheese, shredded

COOKING TIME:

Cooks 12-14 min.

Depending on the type of oven you have this will vary so just look for the cheese to melt and the crust to be browned.

EVERYTHING STYLE PIZZA

Sometimes you just don't know what you want. This particular pizza has a little bit of everything. This way you can appease your taste buds.

SUGGESTED CRUST AND SAUCE:
CRACKER STYLE CRUST – REFER TO PAGE 33 OF PIZZA CRUST SECTION OR CHOOSE THE CRUST OF YOUR CHOICE

CARROT CHILI PASTE SAUCE – REFER TO PAGE 54 OF PIZZA SAUCE SECTION OR CHOOSE THE CRUST OF YOUR CHOICE

TOPPINGS:
½ cup lean ground beef, cooked and drained

1/3 cup Canadian bacon, thinly sliced

1/3 cup pepperoni, thinly sliced

2 cups fresh mushrooms, sliced

2 cups sweet green bell pepper, thinly sliced

2 cups red onion, thinly sliced

2 cups fresh baby spinach

2 tbsp. Kalamata olives, sliced and pitted

1 cup mozzarella cheese, shredded

1 cup cheddar cheese, shredded

COOKING TIME:
Cooks 12-14 min.

Depending on the type of oven you have this will vary so just look for the cheese to melt and the crust to be browned.

GRILLED EVERYTHING STYLE PIZZA

This is one of those sauces that pairs with almost anything. Don't feel like you can't be creative here. Toss some chicken, shrimp, steak and vegetables on your pie and you will wonder why you didn't switch your sauce earlier.

SUGGESTED CRUST AND SAUCE:

THIN CRUST PIZZA CRUST - REFER TO PAGE 31 OF PIZZA CRUST SECTION OR CHOOSE THE CRUST OF YOUR CHOICE

GARLIC AIOLI SAUCE - REFER TO PAGE 64 OF PIZZA SAUCE SECTION OR CHOOSE THE CRUST OF YOUR CHOICE

TOPPINGS:

8 oz. fresh mozzarella, sliced

½ cup roasted peppers, sliced

4 oz. Capicola thinly sliced and torn

1 cup micro greens

1 cup pea shoots

1 cup baby greens

½ bunch fresh basil, torn

COOKING TIME:

Cooks 12-14 min.

Depending on the type of oven you have this will vary so just look for the cheese to melt and the crust to be browned.

CHARTS FOR HOME COOKING

FOOD TEMPERATURES FOR SAFE HEATING, DANGER CHILLING & FREEZING ZONES!

A guide for food temperature cooking!

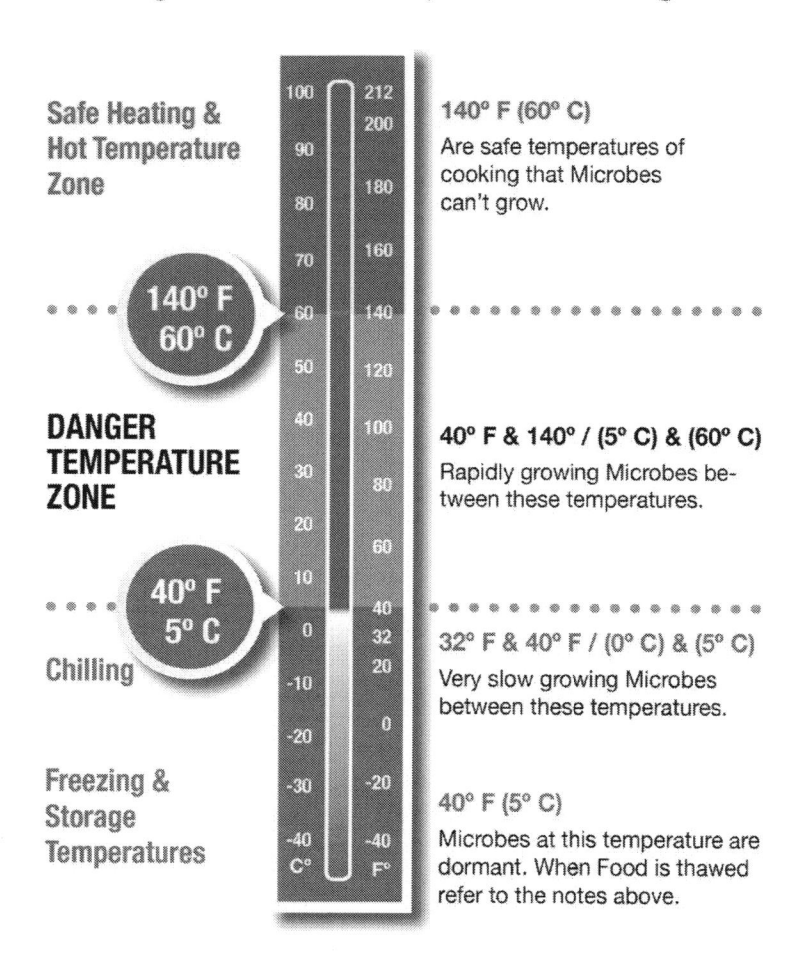

Safe Heating & Hot Temperature Zone

140° F / 60° C

140° F (60° C)
Are safe temperatures of cooking that Microbes can't grow.

DANGER TEMPERATURE ZONE

40° F / 5° C

40° F & 140° / (5° C) & (60° C)
Rapidly growing Microbes between these temperatures.

Chilling

32° F & 40° F / (0° C) & (5° C)
Very slow growing Microbes between these temperatures.

Freezing & Storage Temperatures

40° F (5° C)
Microbes at this temperature are dormant. When Food is thawed refer to the notes above.

MEAT BAKING CHART TEMPERATURES!

BAKING	TEMPERATURE	COOKING TIME
BEEF		
Sirloin or Rib Roast	325 degrees	20-25 minutes
Rump, Round (Roast)	275 degrees	45-50 minutes
VEAL		
Leg, Loin, Rib Roast	325 degrees	35-40 minutes
PORK		
Leg or Loin	325 degrees	20-25 minutes
Crown Roast	325 degrees	15-20 minutes
Shoulder Roast	325 degrees	25-30 minutes
HAM		
Smoked, Pre-Cooked	325 degrees	10-15 minutes
LAMB		
Leg	350-400 degrees	20-25 minutes
Leg, Shoulder Roast	325 degrees	25-30 minutes
Rack (Roast)	400 degrees	20-25 minutes
POULTRY		
Turkey	325 degrees	4-5 hrs / 10-14lbs
Chicken	375 degrees	2.5-3.5hrs / 4-6lbs
Duckling	325-350 degrees	2-3 hrs / 4-5 lbs
Capon	325-350 degrees	2.5-3.5hrs /6-8lbs
Goose	325 degrees	4-5 hrs / 10-12lbs

NEXT ON THE LIST!

HERE'S WHAT YOU DO NOW…

If you were pleased with our book then please leave us a review on amazon where you purchased this book! In the world of an author who writes books independently, your reviews are not only touching but important so that we know you like the material we have prepared for "you" our audience! So, leave us a review…we would love to see that you enjoyed our book!

If for any reason that you were less than happy with your experience then send me an email at **Info@RecipeNerds.com** and let me know how we can better your experience. We always come out with a few volumes of our books and will possibly be able to address some of your concerns. Do keep in mind that we strive to do our best to give you the highest quality of what "we the independent authors" pour our heart and tears into. I am very happy to create new and exciting recipes and do appreciate your purchase. I thank you for your many great reviews and comments!

With a warm heart! ~Leona Stellenberg "Professional Loving Chef"

ABOUT THE AUTHOR

Leona Stellenberg, a true lover of the game of cooking, is an Italian Cuisine Chef with over 15 years of experience in his profession. He is a self-taught, motivated chef that went from preparing a simple meal for a family of 10. But what he didn't realize was that the family was famous and didn't even know it. He was then recommended to others and has been cooking in the homes of other celebrities since that day! Some of his passions include: reading and learning about healthy foods, jogging and now making cookbooks! A motivating story indeed and so are the recipes in this booklet! Enjoy! :)

FREE BOOKS!!!

MAKE SURE YOU GET YOURS!
Monthly We Try Publishing A New Book. Be The First To Get YOUR FREE COPY!

Like receiving free books...I bet you do! We promote our new books to our current members so you can review our new books and give us feedback when we launch new books we are publishing! This helps us determine how we can make our books better for you, our audience! Just go to the url below and leave your name and email. We will send you a complimentary book about once a month.

http://eepurl.com/ds1EjX

Leona Stellenber

CRISPER TRAY PIZZA COOKBOOK RECIPES & NOTES:

Create your very own "Marvelous Masterpieces". Log them in this section. You will be amazed on how many ideas you come up with! Now get creating!

Pizza Name	Crust	Sauce	Toppings

Crisper Tray Pizza Recipe Cookbook

CRISPER TRAY PIZZA COOKBOOK RECIPES & NOTES:

Create your very own "Marvelous Masterpieces". Log them in this section. You will be amazed on how many ideas you come up with! Now get creating!

Pizza Name	Crust	Sauce	Toppings

Printed in Great Britain
by Amazon